BELWIN MASTER
TRUMPET EASY

GRADED SOLOS for the Developing Musician
Composed or Arranged by KEITH SNELL

Volume 2

CONTENTS

Design: Odalis Soto

ORIENTATION

This book is the first of three folios of trumpet duets in the Belwin Master Duets, Volume 2, series. As with the Belwin Master Duets, Volume 1, each of these folios contains a collection of graded duets that should prove to be a useful resource for both the student and the teacher of the trumpet.

Each folio contains transcriptions of works from all periods of music history, arrangements of folk songs and traditional tunes, plus a selection of original compositions by the editor. These duets will provide the beginning student with limited challenges in rhythm, range, and key signatures in music that is both instructive and enjoyable to perform. The teacher will find these duets useful because each has been carefully arranged to develop the student's overall instrumental technique and musicianship.

EASY LEVEL - DUETS

The primary goal of these duets is to provide the beginning trumpet student with the opportunity to develop the technique of playing with and listening to others. In addition, each duet will also present limited challenges in areas of rhythm, range, key signatures and meters. However, greater emphasis is placed on these areas of development in the Intermediate and Advanced volumes of the Belwin Master Duets. As a result, this book can be used by the beginning student at the earliest level of development, since it contains a number of duets that requires the student to be able to play only four or five notes.

It is hoped that these duets will help the beginning trumpet student develop a greater understanding and appreciation of the various musical styles and in doing so, will motivate him or her to explore further as their ability to play the trumpet develops.

Ten Easy Duets For Trumpet

Keith Snell

No. 1

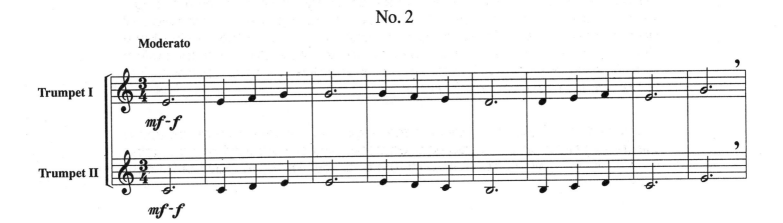

No. 2

No. 3

No. 4

No. 5

No. 6

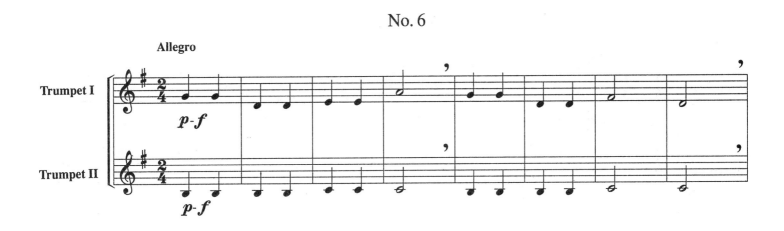

No. 7

Quickly

No. 8

No. 9

Allegretto

No. 10

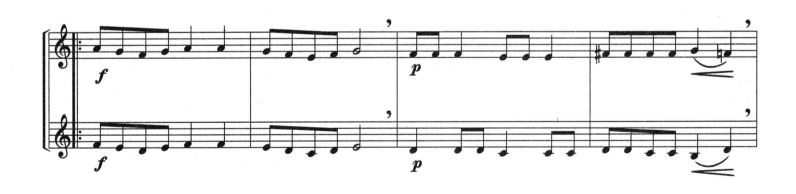

The Carnival

Keith Snell

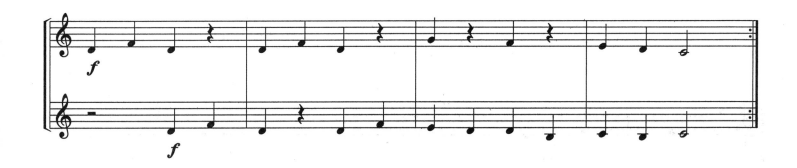

11

The Carman's Whistle

English Renaissance Song

William Byrd (1542-1623)

Evening Song

Keith Snell

Crystal Waltz

Keith Snell

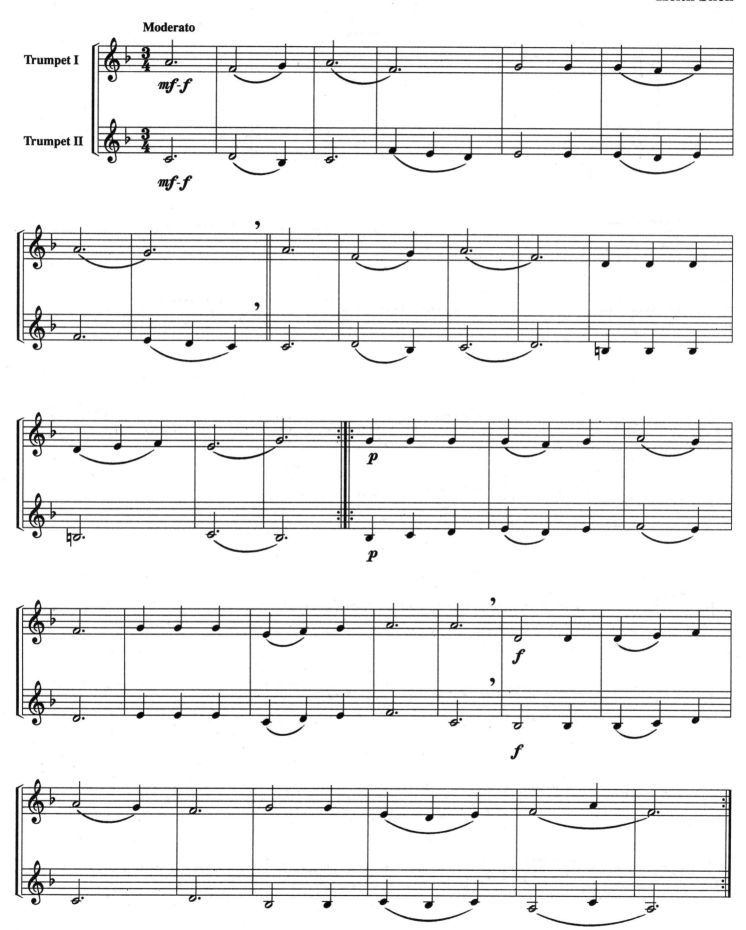

Ecossaise

Ludwig van Beethoven (1770-1827)

Six Fanfares & Flourishes

Keith Snell

No. 1

No. 2

No. 3

No. 4

No. 5

No. 6

Swedish Folk Song

Traditional

Toccata

Keith Snell

Swiss March

Traditional

Rigaudon

Louis Claude Daquin (1694-1772)

Round

William Byrd (1542-1623)

"One And Two And..."

Keith Snell

Processional

Keith Snell

March

Keith Snell

Austrian Dance

Traditional

Little Song

J.S.Bach (1685-1750)